THIS BOOK LOVES YOU

PEWDIEPIE

PENGUIN BOOKS

THIS BOOK LOVES YOU

PewDiePie

A few years ago, it came to my attention on Twitter that a fan had taken one of my tweets and turned it into a beautiful page design. It was of a quote I had written as a parody of all those many pearls of wisdom that the Internet tries to share with the World. And so, I discovered the importance of my great wisdom, and it was clear to me that the World desperately needed my teachings. But was the World ready for such enlightenment?

(Please don't quote this)

I must confess that I have never truly understood the purpose of quotes. If I had listened to half the things that I'm told online, I would not be here today. In fact, if I had listened to the internet, my life would have gone very wrong, very quickly. But still the internet shouts inspirational words at me: 'Happiness', 'Be Strong', 'Positivity', 'Goodness'. Why are strangers taunting me with things I can't have? Who are these sadistic, smug quote-makers?

(Please don't quote this)

And so, for a laugh, I decided to write a book of inspirational quotes . . . a whole book filled with the wisdom of PewDiePie. I hope, perhaps, that this book will motivate, encourage and energize all of you into living your lives to the full? Maybe it will help you to view those inspirational quotes you see on the Internet with a more sceptical eye? Or perhaps you'll just find it a welcome distraction from that difficult bowel movement you're experiencing as you read?

(Please don't quote this)

I hope you enjoy it, but don't try and eat it.
The lasagne version will be released in the near future.

This book was ghostwritten by Edgar.

NeveR

that

BEAUT

FORGET you're IFUL...

compared to A FISH. LIFE IS ALL ABOUT perspective!

MONEY
CAN'T BUY YOU
HAPPINESS

The more

ucks

you give,

the more

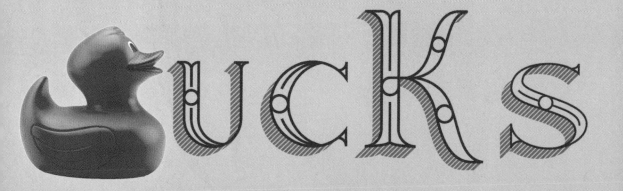

ucks

you lose.

NEVER
GIVE UP
UNLESS YOU'VE TRIED
AT LEAST 3 TIMES
COS
THEN IT'S JUST
IMPOSSIBLE

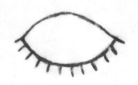

DON'T BE
AFRAID TO SAY
HOW U FEEL,
BECAUSE
NO ONE IS
GOING TO
CARE
ANYWAY.

Roses are Red

Violets are Blue

Eat a C

RUNNING AWAY FROM YOUR PROBLEMS WON'T MAKE YOU SKINNY.

YELLOW IS EVIL
SO DON'T DRINK
YOUR OWN...

IF YOU CAN

FIGHT

YOUR WAY OUT

★★★★ ★★★★ OF A ★★★★ ★★★★

SITUATION

DON'T,

★★★★ ★★★★★

YOU'LL DIE!

Things ~~can~~ WILL always get worse.

To fly, you must get rid of the things that weigh you down.

This is why all your friends left you.

NOTHING IN LIFE COMES EASY

SO WHY DO YOU EXPECT SOMETHING OUT OF A QUOTE

PERFECTION IS SOMETHING UNATTAINABLE

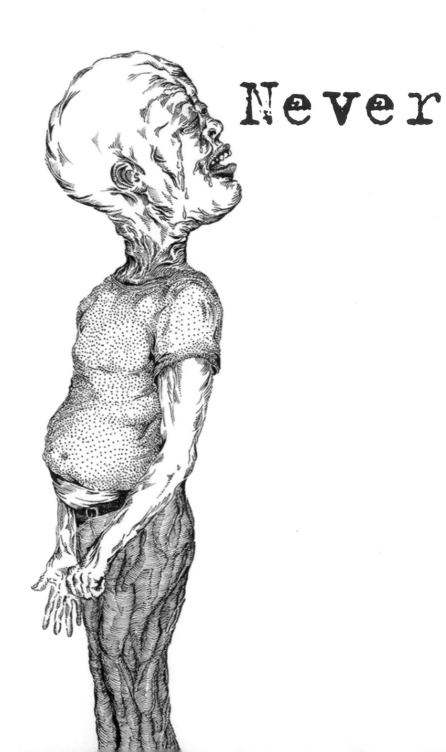

Never

look back.

If life doesn't go right

take a left...

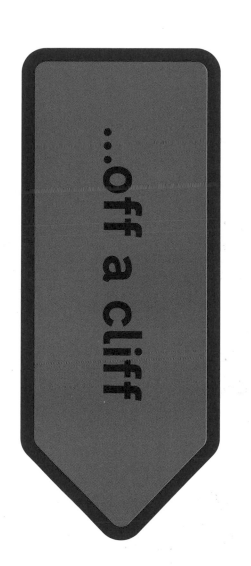

DON'T KILL ANYONE. PEOPLE DIE IF THEY GET KILLED

Everyone is entitled
to their own opinion

F

even though

THEY'RE UCKING WRONG!!

LIFE IS ABOUT LISTENING TO QUOTES THAT RELATE TO YOU, SO YOU CAN FEEL MOMENTARILY BETTER ABOUT YOURSELF. HERE'S A PICTURE OF A . . .

DUCK

YOUR PET
ONLY LOVES
YOU BECAUSE
YOU GIVE
IT FOOD

DON'T BE YOURSELF, BE A PIZZA

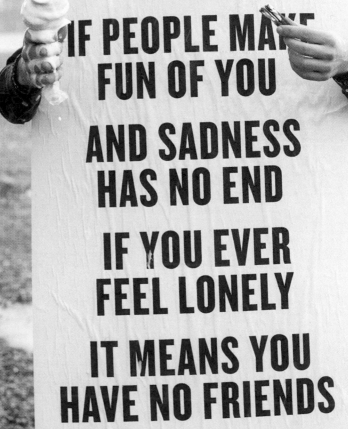

Don't
be a
Bitch

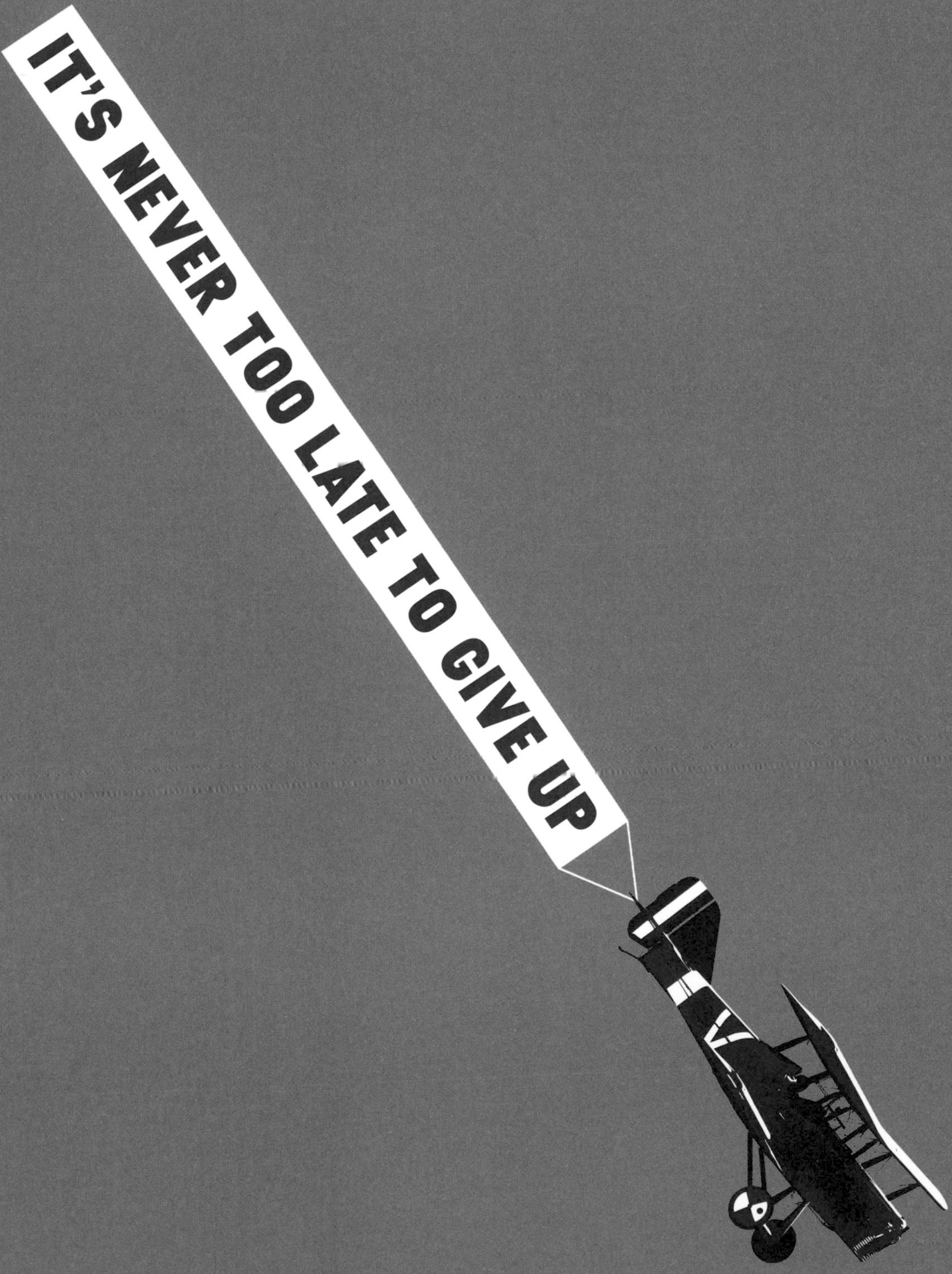
IT'S NEVER TOO LATE TO GIVE UP

Don't
sugar coat
everything . . .

you'll get
diabetes.

Impossible is nothing.
Doing nothing is easy.

DON'T SELL YOURSELF SHORT . . .

UNLESS YOU NEED
QUICK MONEY.

HEY, I'M NOT JUDGING.

LET'S
FACE IT,
YOU'LL
NEVER
BE AS
COOL
AS THIS.

IF YOU EVER TAKE ADVICE FROM A **DUCK,** REMEMBER: **DON'T. DUCKS CAN'T TALK.** YOU'RE PROBABLY ON DRUGS.

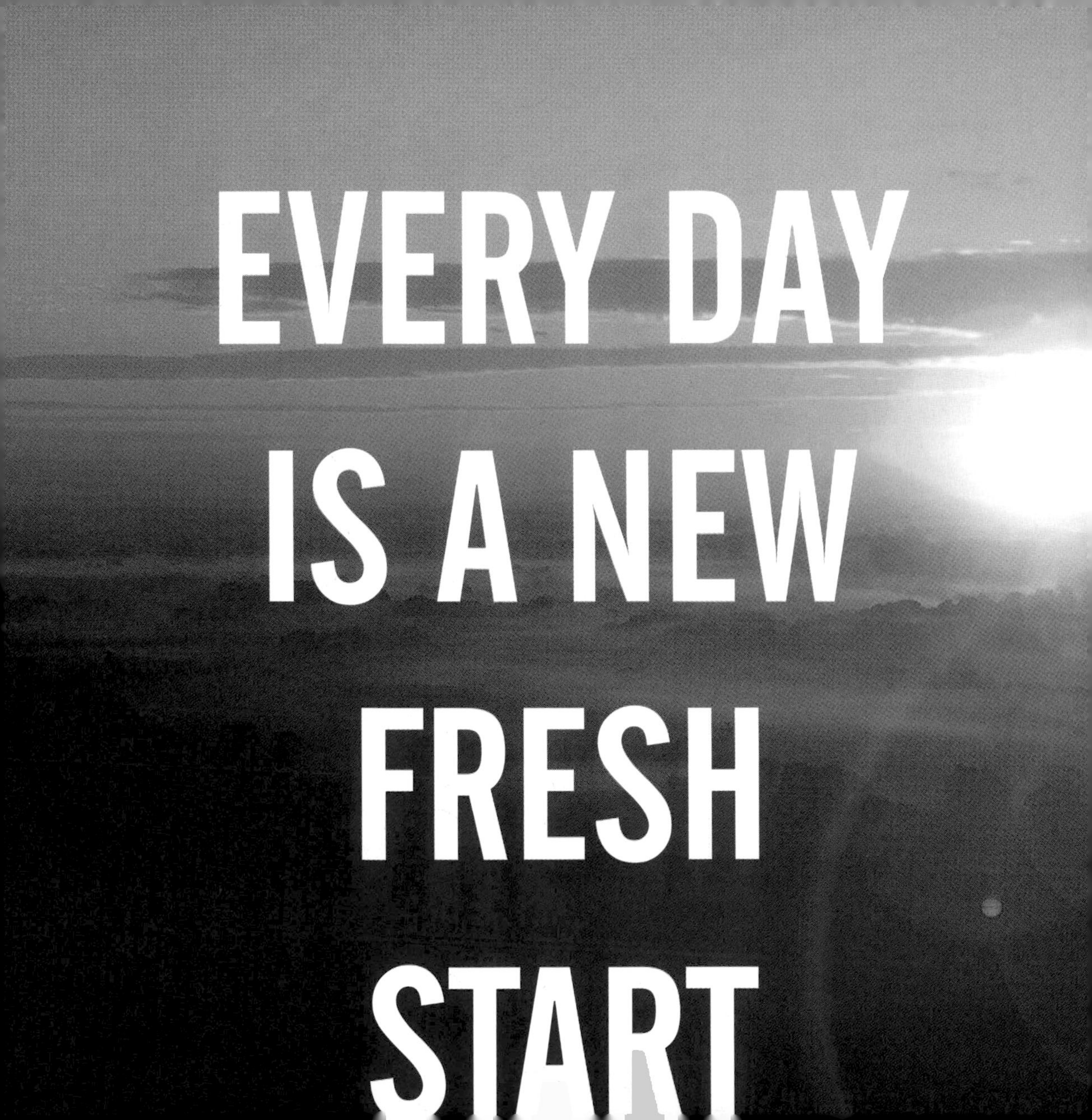
EVERY DAY
IS A NEW
FRESH
START

TO GO STRAIGHT BACK TO BED

IF YOU EVER FEEL SAD, JUST REMEMBER: EVEN UNICORNS PROBABLY HAVE DIARRHOEA EVERY ONCE IN A WHILE.

YOU CAN'T~~WIN THE RACE~~
~~**BY NOT TRYING**~~
by cutting off their legs.

MONDAY IS COMING!

LOADING . . .

Running Out
OF Money
DOESN'T COUNT
as EXERCISE.

Without WINTER, you can't fully appreciate the beauty of SUMMER.

Without you, I can
appreciate
so many things.

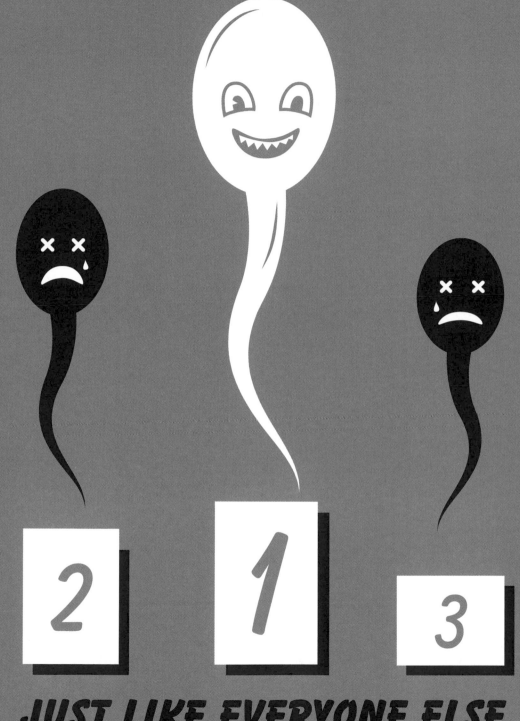

JUST LIKE EVERYONE ELSE.

DO YOU REMEMBER ALL THE EMBARRASSING MOMENTS YOU'VE HAD? DON'T WORRY, I'LL REMIND YOU.
– BRAIN

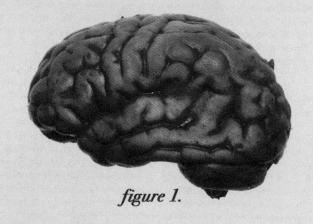

figure 1.

YOU

CAN

NEVER

FAIL

IF

YOU

NEVER

SO WHY BOTHER.

TRY

THERE CAN'T BE WINNERS WITHOUT LOSERS

SO REALLY YOU'RE DOING THE WORLD A FAVOUR.

YOU CAN'T

YOU CAN'T

STOP CROSSING MY TEXTS

YOU CAN'TUNT

smile*

*it makes you look like a psychopath

IF YOU

EVER FEEL

DOWN . . .

JUST REMEMBER:

NO ONE ELSE IS

ABOVE YOU.

IF YOU WEAR

IF YOU'RE ROUND, YOU MIGHT NOT BE IN SHAPE

BUT AT LEAST YOU ARE A SHAPE

Don't waste time loving someone who doesn't love you back.

Love ducks.

Ducks always love you back.

HATERS GONNA HATE

DUCKS GONNA QUACK

THEY SAY LOVE IS BLIND

IT'S EITHER THAT OR YOU'LL HAVE TO DATE A BLIND PERSON.

**LIFE IS A DEATH
SENTENCE AND
YOU SHOULD
RESENT YOUR
PARENTS.**

———

Quotes are the most important thing in the universe, and you should always take them to heart.

———

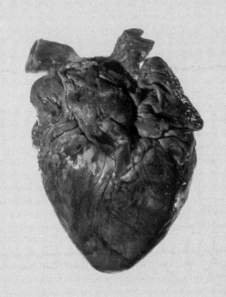

Backflipping constantly is a great way to

If someone hates your guts

feed it to them.

If someone loves your guts

they're probably a zombie.

The *Secret* to a *Happy* *Life* is::

P.T.O →

YOU SERIOUSLY EXPECTED TO FIND IT IN THIS BOOK? HAHAHA

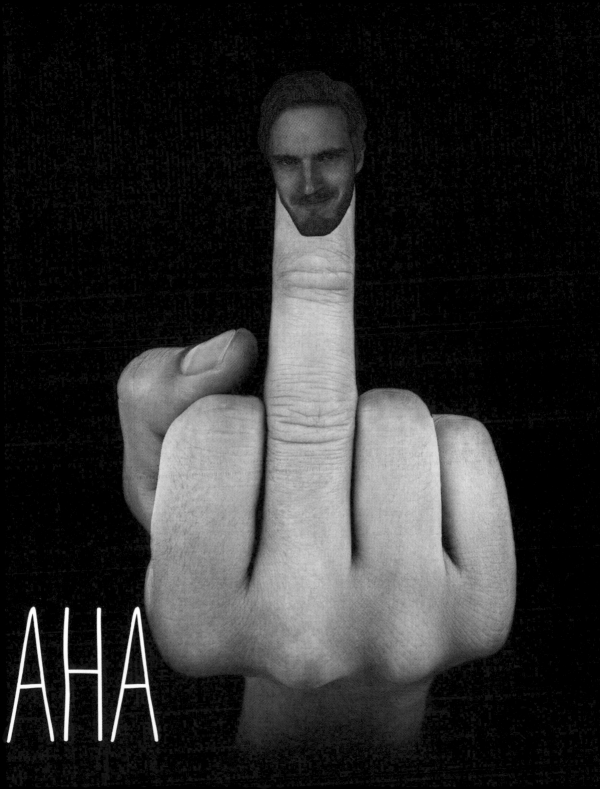

AHA

JUST
BECAUSE
YOU HAVE
AN
OPINION

DOESN'T MEAN ANYONE HAS TO GIVE A DUCK

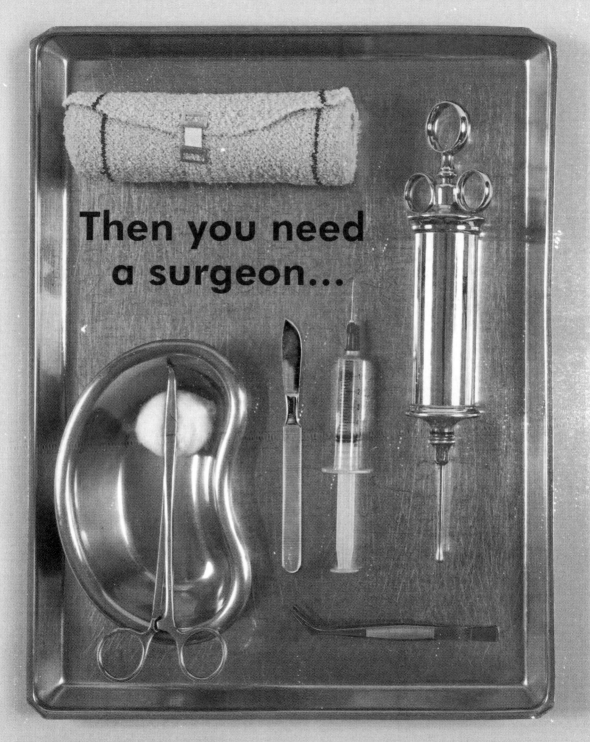

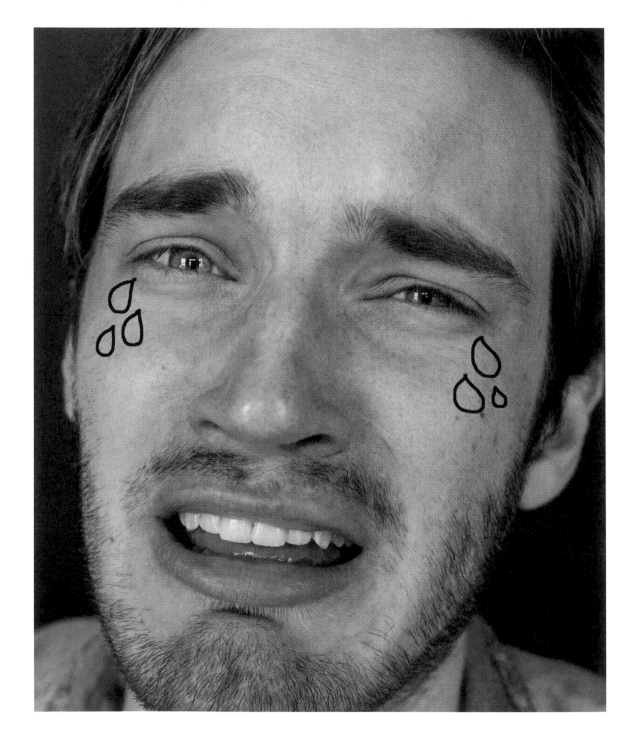

Life without nipples would be pointless.

— Duck

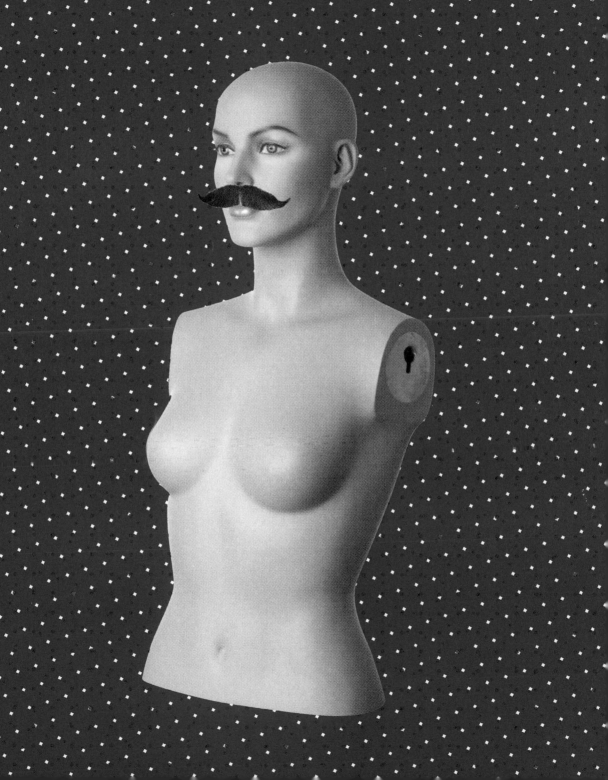

WITHOUT NIPPLES, BOOBS WOULD JUST BE

BUTT CHEEKS THAT DON'T POOP.

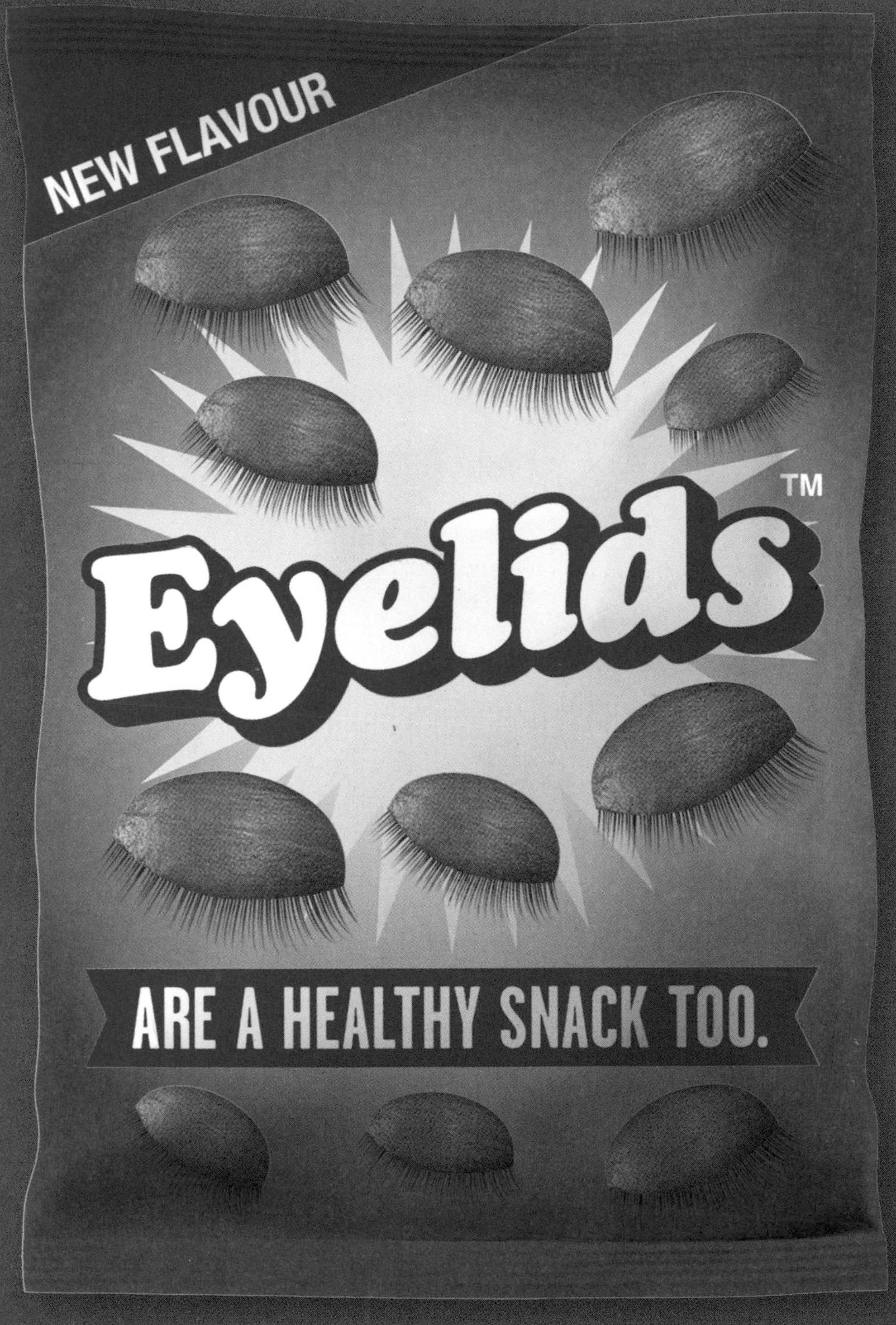
NEW FLAVOUR
Eyelids™
ARE A HEALTHY SNACK TOO.

RESIST EATING YOUR KIDS. THEY CAN DO ALL YOUR CHORES FOR YOU.

-DUCK

NEVER
REGRET
ANY-
THING.

*Except that awkward emo faze you went through.

Hide your tears;
pretend you are ok.
Crying in the shower
camouflages them away.

IF YOU CAN'T AFFORD TO BUY THIS BOOK

OPTION 1: DID YOU STEAL IT?

OPTION 2: SELL YOUR KIDNEY?

OPTION 3: OFFER YOUR SOUL?

DON'T BE A SALAD, BE THE BEST GODDAMN BROCCOLI YOU COULD EVER BE.

Duck

Loves

you

THIS

much.

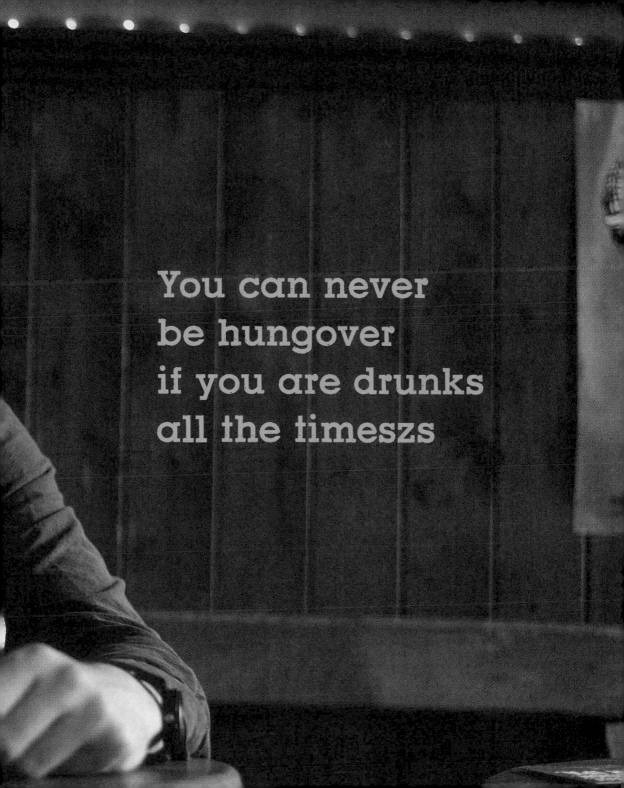

You can never
be hungover
if you are drunks
all the timeszs

THERE'S ALWAYS A NEW DAY TOMORROW

'SHERLOCK'

DON'T BE SOMETHING YOU'RE NOT.
UNLESS YOU CAN BE A FABULOUS UNICORN.
ALWAYS BE A FABULOUS UNICORN.

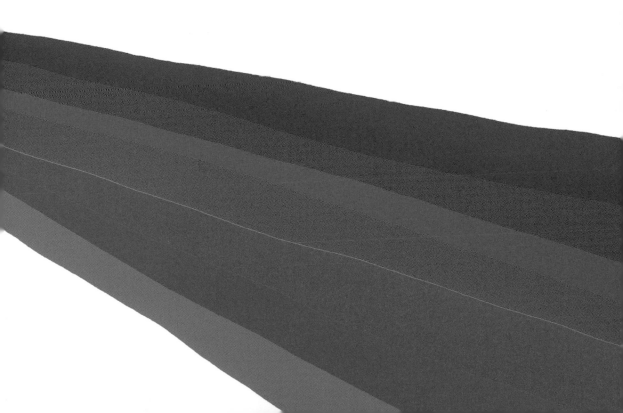

Success is never an accident,
which is why it will never happen to you.

If you can't beat 'em, eat 'em.

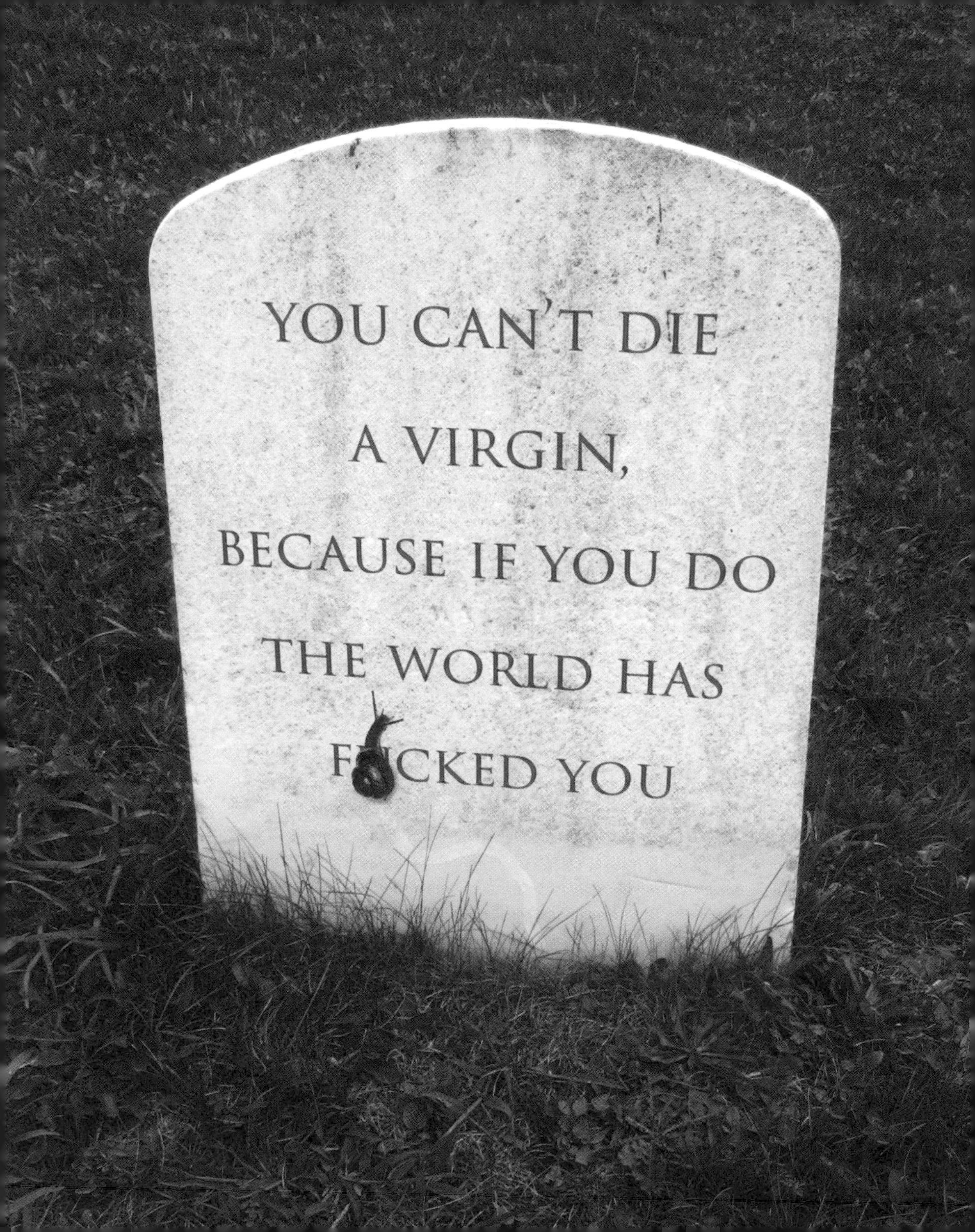
YOU CAN'T DIE
A VIRGIN,
BECAUSE IF YOU DO
THE WORLD HAS
F CKED YOU

EVERYTHING HAPPENS FOR A REASON.
YES, EVEN THAT AWKWARD RASH YOU HAVE.

MONDAY	TUESDAY	WEDNESDAY	THURS
~~4~~	~~5~~	6	7
11	12 EVERY	13 DAY	~~14~~
18	19	20	21
25 BLOODY HELL	26	27	28 H MA

	FRIDAY	SATURDAY	SUNDAY
	1 EVERY	**2** DAY	**3** IS A
	8 SECOND	**9** CHAN	**10** CE
	15 YOU	**16** STILL	**17** FAIL
	22	**23**	**24**
	29 CHANGES	**30** DO YOU	**31** NEED

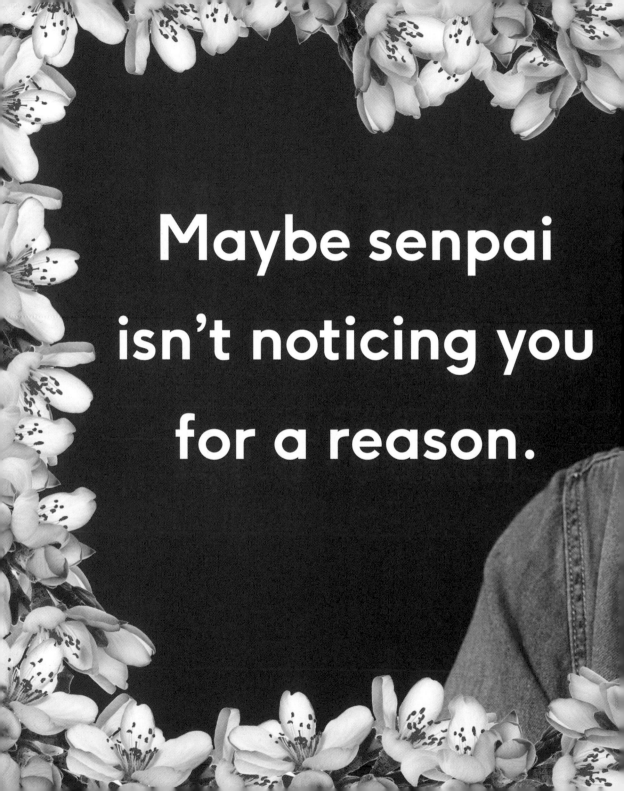

Maybe senpai isn't noticing you for a reason.

DO

OR EVER

NEVER

ANYTHING

YOU'RE WELCOME

If life sucks, get a straw and show life who's boss.

TREAT PEOPLE WHO
BELIEVE IN KARMA BADLY.
THEY OBVIOUSLY HAD
IT COMING.

YOU'RE NOT BAD

EVERYONE ELSE IS JUST SO MUCH BETTER

I prayed for beauty ...
it worked.

Don't you forget about me.*

*Cos if you do I'll burn your f@%king house down.

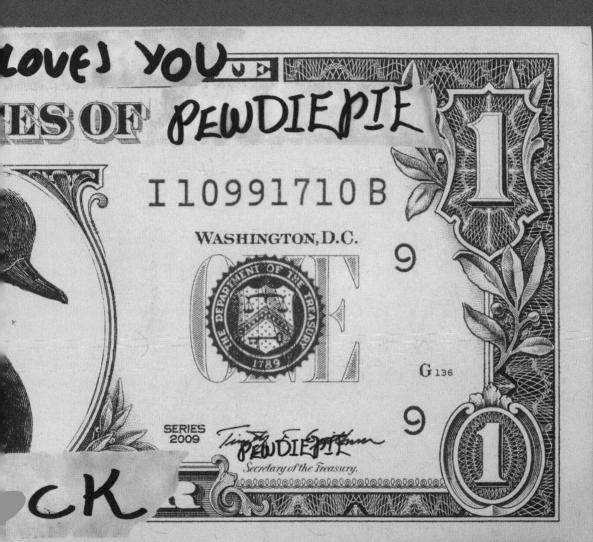

Unless you have a face tattoo.

Then you are screwed for life.

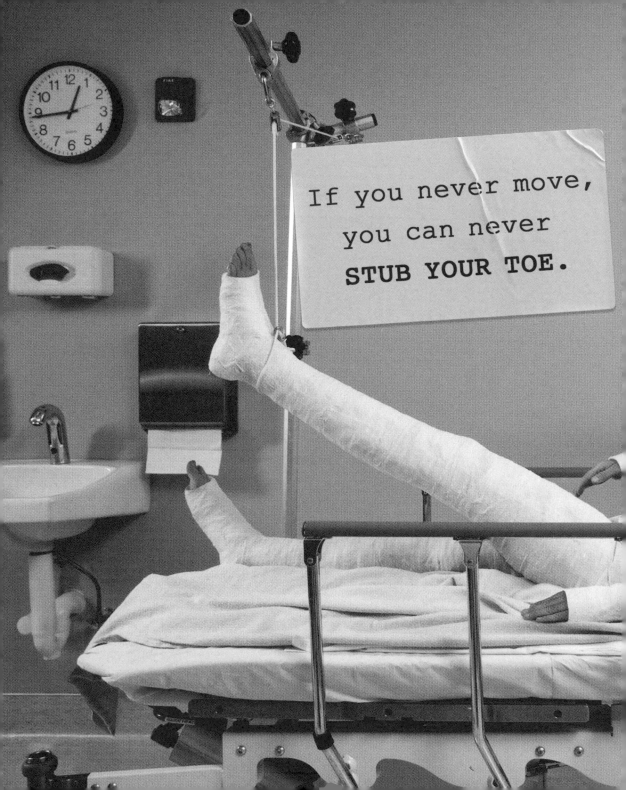

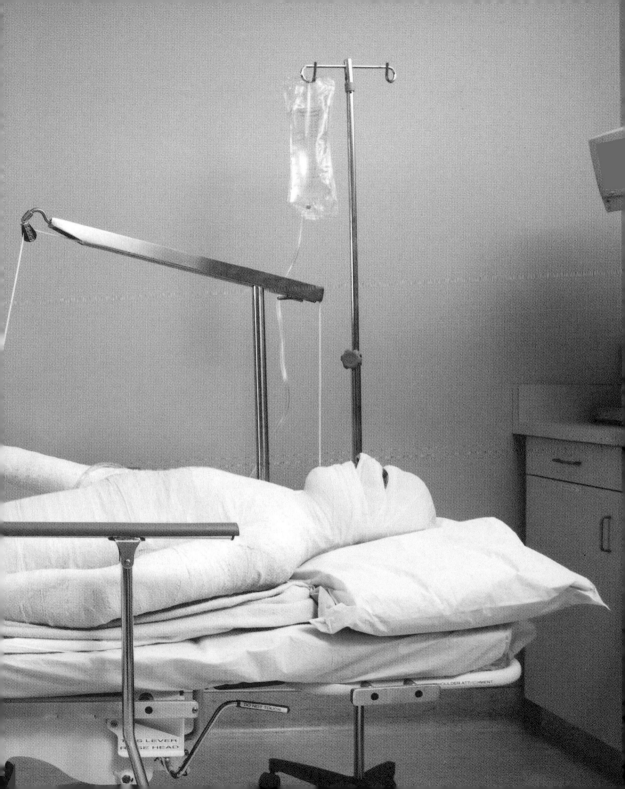

Embrace your missteak.

You can't make
everyone happy.

So focus on making
yourself happy so
that maybe one
day your happiness
will evolve and
EAT EVERYONE.

Don't listen to haters.

Live your life the way
you want to live it.

It's important to love yourself.

Because no one else does.

To Pew Die Pie
love you lott
Pew Die Pie
xxx

NOW
ROCK
BOTTOM

KEEP YOUR FRIENDS CLOSE

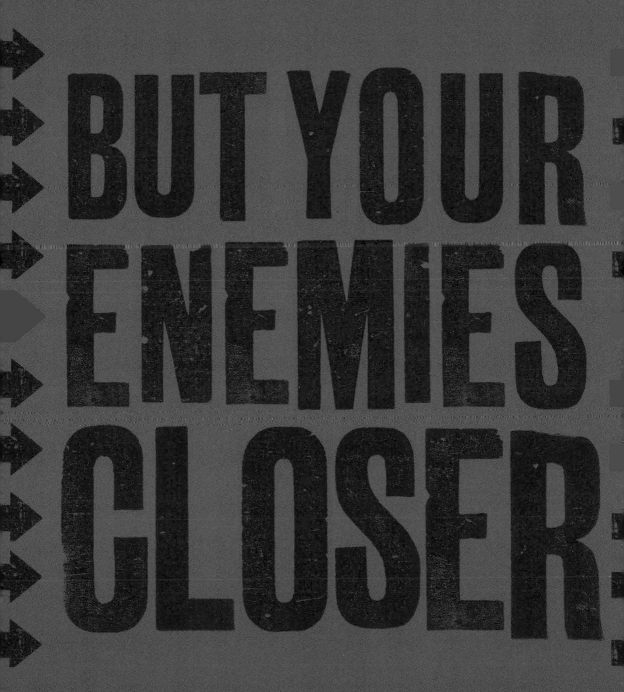

UNLESS YOU DON'T HAVE ANY FRIENDS

THEN JUST SIT IN A CORNER AND CRY

IF YOU DON'T WIN, YOU LOSE . . .

LAST

Just checking to see if you knew.

WHAT

DOESN'T

KILL

YOU

MAKES...
YOU
STRONG
ER

YOU MAY NOT BE STRONG.
YOU MAY NOT BE GOOD ENOUGH.
YOU MAY NEVER EVEN
BE A DECENT PERSON.

I FORGET THE REST...

PewDiePie say:

Don't give up, because if you do, you're seriously such a pussy.

Never give up on those dreams of yours… and stuff.

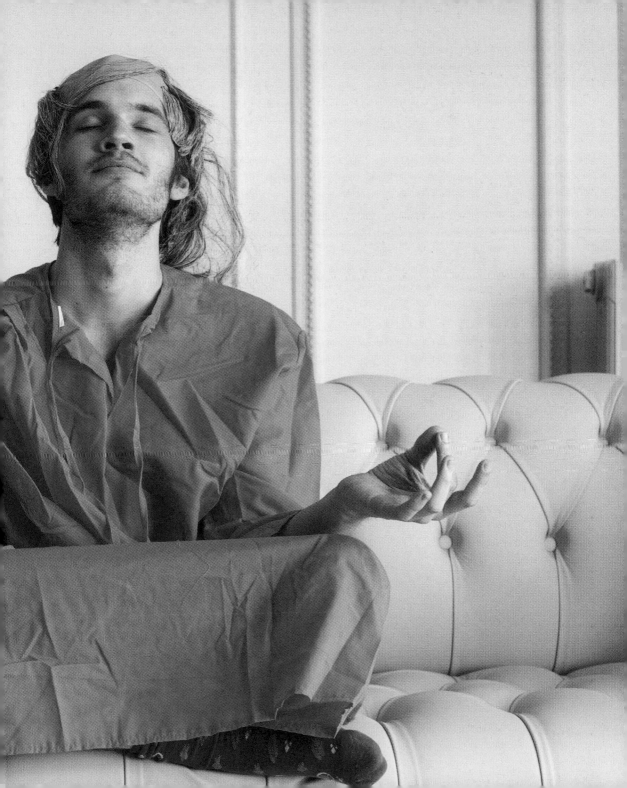

KEEP CALM

Just remember to breathe

you dumb blondie.

NEVER, NEVER
GIVE
UP

COMPLAIN.

DEMAND TO SEE
A MANAGER.
GET
LIFE FIRED
AND RUIN LIFE'S LIFE.
REALISE YOUR LIFE
IS NOW EMPTY.

DON'T WO
YOUR PI
IF YOU EN
TOMORRO
ALL B

RRY ABOUT
OBLEMS.
UP DEAD
N, THEY'LL
GONE.

-DUCK

GIVE A MAN A FISH AND YOU FEED HIM FOR A DAY. BECOME A FISH AND BE HIS L♡VER 4 LIFE.

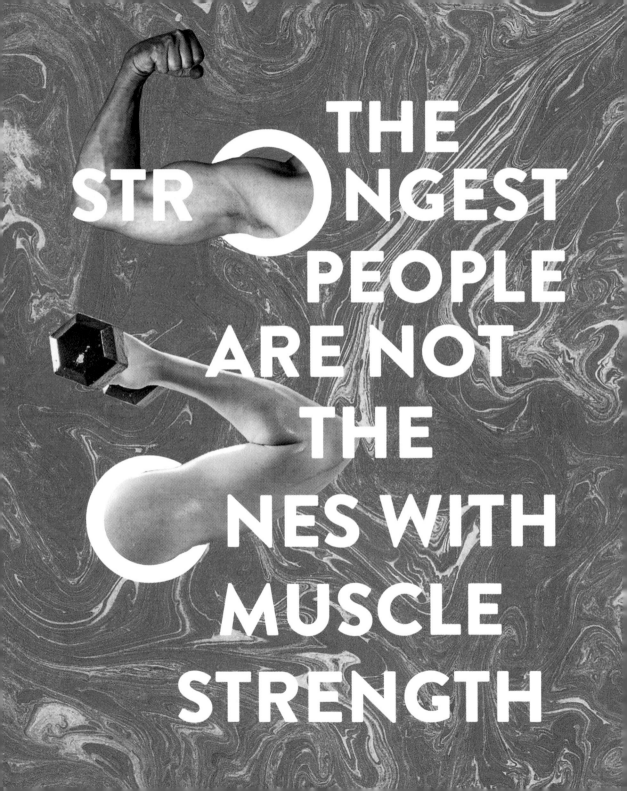

THE STRONGEST PEOPLE ARE NOT THE ONES WITH MUSCLE STRENGTH

DON'T USE TAMPONS IF YOU'RE A BOY

-A Wise Man

THIS IS YOU

EVERY SECOND YOU'RE CLOSER TO OBLIVION. NO QUOTE IN THE WORLD IS GONNA CHANGE THAT.

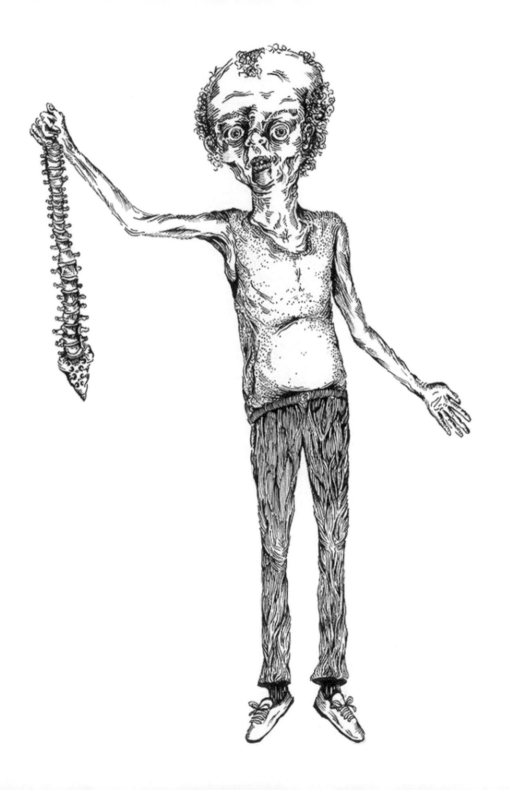

Don't
let
things
hold
you back.

JUST BE YOURSELF!

WHAT THE HELL WERE YOU THINKING?!

I WANT TO BE THE
ONE WHO CATCHES
YOU WHEN YOU FALL.

– FLOOR

If you're wrong 100% of the time,
you're right 0% of the time.
A wiseman said that.
Spoiler: it was me.

YOU HAVE TO BE REAL
WITH YOURSELF
BEFORE YOU CAN BE
REAL WITH SOMEONE ELSE

AND YOU
REALLY SUCK

IF YOU CAN'T
BEAT THEM,
THERE'S STILL
A GOOD CHANCE
TO ANNOY THEM.

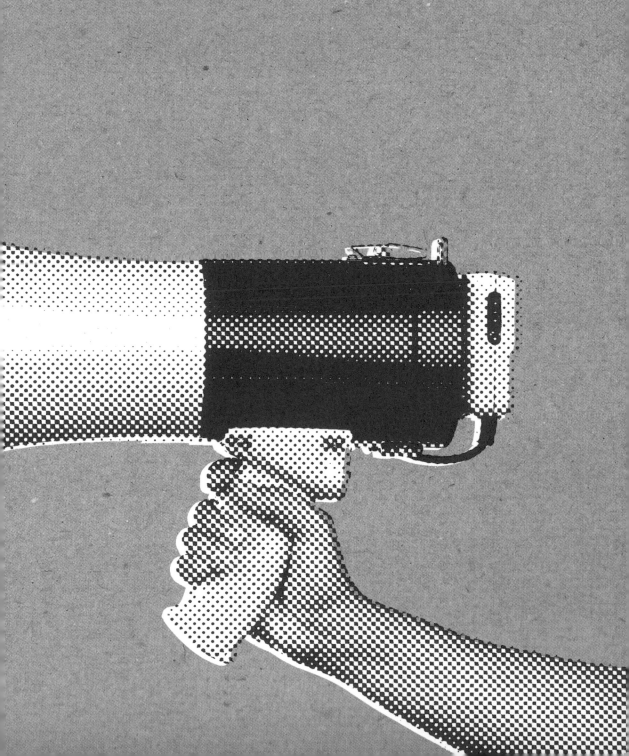

WAYS INSPIRATIONAL QUOTES ARE USED

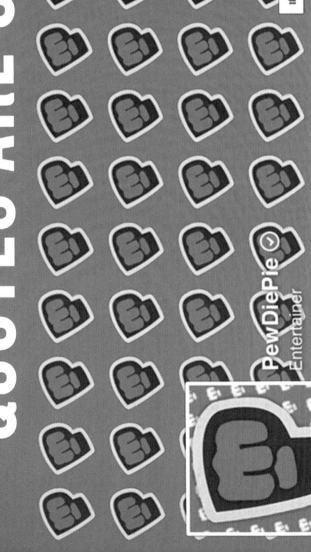

PewDiePie ✓
Entertainer

Timeline   About   Photos   Likes   More ▾

👍 Like   + Follow   ➜ Share   •••

📝 Post   📷 Photo/Video

98% TO POST ON FACEBOOK TO FEEL BETTER ABOUT YOURSELF

Post

6.2m people like this

👤 Invite friends to like this Page

? Ask for PewDiePie's website

PHOTOS

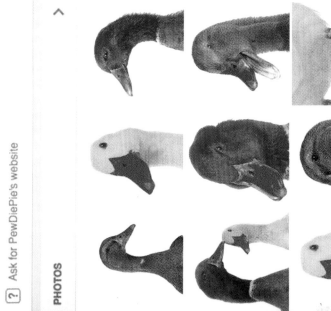

PewDiePie updated his cover photo.
7 July at 00:38 ·

1% FOR THE POSITIVE DEVELOPMENT OF PEOPLE'S LIVES

Like   Comment   Share

112,154 others like this.

227 shares

View previous comments

1% FOR THIS BOOK TO **CRAP ON**

49 mins · Like

Write a comment...

PewDiePie with 38 others

THANKS TO THE BROS

Biggest thanks to Marzia! And big thanks to Amy and Kevin Finnerty, Sarah Wick, and everyone at Maker Studios; Alex Clarke, Ben Schrank, Casey McIntyre, Hattie Adam-Smith, Francesca Russell, Elyse Marshall, John Hamilton and his design team, Matt Carr, Susan Bell, photographer, and everyone at Penguin Books; all the bros; the pugs; and lastly to Duck.

PENGUIN BOOKS

UK | USA | Canada | Ireland | Australia
India | New Zealand | South Africa

Penguin Books is part of the Penguin Random House group of companies
whose addresses can be found at global.penguinrandomhouse.com.

First published 2015

005

Colour reproduction by Rhapsody
Printed in Italy by L.E.G.O. S.p.a

A CIP catalogue record for this book is available from the British Library

ISBN: 978–1–405–92438–2

www.greenpenguin.co.uk

MIX
Paper from
responsible sources
FSC® C018179

Penguin Random House is committed to a
sustainable future for our business, our readers
and our planet. This book is made from Forest
Stewardship Council® certified paper.

PICTURE CREDITS

Photography © Susan Bell: 5, 16, 21, 37, 44, 50–51, 54–5, 63, 71, 100–101, 120, 124–5, 132–3, 135, 140–41, 146–7, 150–51, 156–7, 166–7, 172, 177, 182–3, 194, 198–9, 213, 226–7, 236.

Grateful acknowledgement is made by the publisher for permission to reproduce the images on the following pages:

2–3 © Shutterstock; 10–11 © plainpicture/ponton and © Mary Evans/Classic Stock/H. Armstrong Roberts; 17 © Tim Hawley/Getty Images; 18–19 © Attck; 22–23 © Linda Steward/Getty Images; 25 © Viktor Flumé, © Getty Images; 26–7 © iStock.com/photka, © iStock.com/spawns; 29 © Tobi Corney/Getty Images; 39 © iStock.com/Rtimages, © iStock.com/eelnosiva; 48–9 © Sebastian Marmaduke/Image Source; 52–3; 56 © Warren Photographic; 60–61 © iStock.com/Korovin, ©iStock.com/Ridofranz, © IStock/Noppol Mahawanjam; 62 © iStock.com/egal, © iStock.com/GlobalP, © iStock.com/CoreyFord; 64–5 © iStock.com/GlobalStock; 66–7 © iStock.com/PeopleImages, © Oriontrail/Shutterstock, © iStock.com/GlobalP, © iStock.com/camdoc3; 68 © Daniel Day/Getty Images; 70 © iStock.com/ViewApart; 74–5 © iStock.com/Nata_Slavetskaya; © iStock.com/Lambros Kazan, © iStock.com/Oksanita; 78–9; 82–3 © Sarah Lynn Paige/Getty Images, © Shebeko/Shutterstock; 86 © mikeledray/Shutterstock; 87 © Getty Images; 88 © fridhelm/Shutterstock; 90 © CSA Images/Color Printstock Collection/Getty Images; 91 © Image Source/Getty Images; 94 © fStop Images GmbH/Alamy; 95 © Victor Albrow/Getty Images; 98–9 © iStock.com/mazzzur; 104 © Angus Hamilton; 105 © Getty Images; 107 © PM Images/Getty Images; 108–9 © Chelsea Kedron/Geety Images; 115 © Christian Adams/Getty Images; 118 © Belovodchenko Anton/Shutterstock; 119 © Image Source/Getty Images, © Shutterstock; 123 © iStock.com/zakazpc; 126–7 © Piotr Marcinski/Shutterstock; 129 © iStock.com/CSA-Printstock; 137 © iStock.com/vuk8691, © iStock.com/Creativeye99; 142–3 © Rtimages/Shutterstock, © urchyks/Shutterstock; 151 © Peter Dazeley/Getty Images; 152 © iStock.com/lisinski; 156–7 © Shutterstock; 160–61 © iStock.com/GlobalP, © iStock.com/kirstypargeter; 168–9 © iStock.com/jorgeantonio; 170–71 © Pawel Michalowski/Shutterstock; 174–5 © John Lund/Getty Images; 180 © Mark Murphy/Getty Images; 184–5 © Felix Kjellberg; 190 © DEBROCKE/Corbis; 191 © Peter Dazeley/Getty Images; 197 © chaoss/Shutterstock; 200 © Ron Levine/Getty Images, © Steve Mcsweeny/Getty Images; 201 © Shutterstock; 216 © iStock.com/Yuri_Arcurs; 218–19 © VICTOR HABBICK VISIONS/Getty Images, © Nadiia Ishchenko/Shutterstock; 222 © Angela Wyant/Getty Images; 224 © Maria Toutoudaki/Getty Image; 225 © EVERSOFINE/Getty Images; 228 © CSA Images/Getty Images; 229 © Milena Milani/Shutterstock; 230–31 © iStock.com/manley099.

Illustration © Kevin Long: 40–41, 138–9, 220–21 and © Ian Stevenson: 14–15, 144–5, 153, 162.

Every effort has been made to attain the correct image permissions, however any omissions will be corrected in future editions.

I
LiED